GIANTS

by

Rebecca Phillips-Bartlett

Minneapolis, Minnesota

Credits
All images are courtesy of Shutterstock.com, unless otherwise specified. With thanks to Getty Images, Thinkstock Photo, iStockphoto, and Adobe Stock.

Recurring – klayksun, Macrovector, kenyaa. Cover – artyway, Dn Br, 4th Design. 4–5 – iobard, Morphart Creation, tomertu. 6–7 – Daniel Eskridge, IanGoodPhotography. 8–9 – Chipmunk131, Dmitr1ch, shrimpgraphic, Marek Tr, Christos Georghiou, tynyuk, IG Digital Arts, Aunt Spray. 10–11 – DomCritelli, NextMarsMedia, Tithi Luadthong. 12–13 – prapann, Tithi Luadthong, Duangkamon Panyapatiphan, Gorodenkoff. 14–15 – Marti Bug Catcher, Tithi Luadthong, Triff, Warm_Tail, hapabapa. 16–17 – David Tadevosian, DeStefano, Peter Porrini. 18–19 – Vincentuilll, Warpaint, mauribo. 20–21 – Lyd Photography, Michael Xiaos, Mihai Simonia, Divaneth-Dias, mylasa. 22–23 – sunabesyou, vectorfusionart.

Bearport Publishing Company Product Development Team
Publisher: Jen Jenson; Director of Product Development: Spencer Brinker; Managing Editor: Allison Juda; Editor: Cole Nelson; Associate Editor: Naomi Reich; Associate Editor: Tiana Tran; Art Director: Colin O'Dea; Designer: Kim Jones; Designer: Kayla Eggert; Product Development Specialist: Owen Hamlin

Library of Congress Cataloging-in-Publication Data

Names: Phillips-Bartlett, Rebecca, 1999- author.
Title: Giants / Rebecca Phillips-Bartlett.
Description: Fusion books. | Minneapolis, MN : Bearport Publishing Company, [2025] | Series: Mythical creatures | Includes index.
Identifiers: LCCN 2024033534 (print) | LCCN 2024033535 (ebook) | ISBN 9798892327404 (library binding) | ISBN 9798892327909 (paperback) | ISBN 9798892328272 (ebook)
Subjects: LCSH: Giants (Folklore)--Juvenile literature.
Classification: LCC GR560 .P52 2025 (print) | LCC GR560 (ebook) | DDC 398.21--dc23/eng/20240724
LC record available at https://lccn.loc.gov/2024033534
LC ebook record available at https://lccn.loc.gov/2024033535

For more information, write to Bearport Publishing, 5357 Penn Avenue South, Minneapolis, MN 55419.

CONTENTS

MYTHS, MAGIC, AND MORE

Most people have heard of the huge creatures with humanlike bodies known as giants. But you probably haven't seen one in real life. Why not? Because giants are **mythical** creatures!

For thousands of years, people from all over the world have told stories about giants. Different **legends** talk about the creatures in different ways. Let's learn what the stories have to say!

The Vikings believed giants were the very first beings to exist.

WHAT DOES A GIANT LOOK LIKE?

Let's take a look at these oversized beasts.

Clothes

Most giants from stories wear scruffy clothes.

Feet

Huge feet may help giants support their tall bodies.

Weapons
Legends say giants use many kinds of weapons, including swords and spears.
Body
The body of a giant looks like a human's. In some **myths**, a giant can turn into an animal, too!

A TOWERING CREATURE

What's the biggest thing to know about giants? Obviously, it's their height!

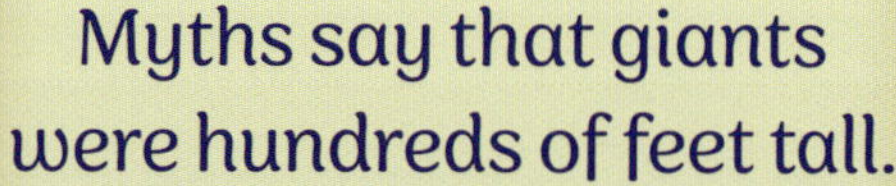

Myths say that giants were hundreds of feet tall.

Mammoths

Giants would need strong bones to support their tall bodies. Long ago, large bones were found buried in the ground. But scientists believe they belonged to mammoths.

Goliath

In stories, Goliath was a warrior who was about 9 feet (3 m) tall.

Finn McCool

An Irish giant named Finn McCool moved rocks and reshaped the land.

Atlas

Legends say the Greek giant Atlas held the sky on his shoulders.

ELEMENTAL POWERS

Apart from towering heights, what else have we heard about these mythical creatures? Different types of giants have different powers.

Legends say frost giants sometimes change the weather. They could make it extremely cold and harsh.

A frost giant

A fire giant

When angry, fire giants are said to make **volcanoes** erupt. Most eruptions are actually caused by melted rock building up under Earth's surface.

Many people think of forests as **healing**. Could forest giants have that power, too? Maybe they use it to help other giants and even some humans.

A forest giant

THIS AND THAT

According to Greek legends, some giants can never die. Some animals have similar lives. The **immortal** jellyfish can restart its life by turning young again. This means it cannot die from old age.

Immortal jellyfish

Many giants from stories make weapons from natural materials. Scientists found that the oldest weapons made by humans were spears. These early spears were just sharp sticks!

Stories claim some fire giants fight with flaming swords. Today, most swords are made from steel.

SHAPING THE LAND

Many tales tell that giants shape the land we live on. However, scientists have other explanations. . . .

Does the heavy weight of giants cause earthquakes? Not quite. Earthquakes are created by the movement of huge, underground rocks.

Some say lakes formed from giants' footprints. However, many lakes were actually carved out by **glaciers**. Then, the ice melted to fill the holes with water.

WHERE GIANTS LIVE

According to many legends, giants lived long ago in **ancient** Greece. They were said to leave their mark in nature. Could the sound of thunder mean there is a giant nearby?

Thunder is actually the sound created by a flash of lightning.

Myths say that when Irish giant Finn McCool got angry, he threw huge rocks into the sea. These piled rocks became the Giant's Causeway. Scientists today know the rocky area was made by a volcano.

The Giant's Causeway

MYTHICAL LOOK-ALIKES

There are other mythical creatures like giants. Let's look at a few.

Ogres (OH-gurz) are mythical creatures similar to giants in their large build. But unlike giants, ogres are thought to eat humans.

An ogre

The Yeti (YET-tee) is a mythical creature that lives in the Himalayan mountains. This beast is thought to have long white fur. Many legends say the Yeti looks like a mix of a large human and an ape.

Yeti

Bear footprints in the snow are often mistaken for the Yeti's.

REAL-LIFE GIANTS?

Where do the stories of giants come from? Maybe from old bones. . . .

A dinosaur's bones

A mammoth's bones

Bones

Big bones buried underground were thought to belong to giants. Scientists later realized those were the bones of large animals, such as elephants, mammoths, and even dinosaurs!

Fake Skeletons

More than 20 years ago, someone posted pictures on the internet of a **skeleton** with huge bones. People thought it was the skeleton of a giant. However, it was later found out the photos were fake.

MYSTERIOUS MYTHICAL CREATURES

Giants are fun, mysterious creatures. We can learn a lot from stories about these big beasts.

If you can't get enough of giants, just read some books! There is so much to explore about these magical, mythical creatures.

GLOSSARY

ancient belonging to a time long ago

glaciers huge pieces of ice and snow

healing becoming healthy again

immortal living or lasting forever

legends stories from the past that may have a mix of truth and made-up things

mythical based on stories or something made up in the imagination

myths old stories that tell of strange or magical events and creatures

skeleton the bones of an animal that protect or support its body

volcanoes mountains that can send out rocks, ash, and lava in sudden explosions

INDEX